DISCARD

MACHINES FOR YOU

MACHINES FOR YOU

by F. WENDEROTH SAUNDERS

Illustrated by the Author

Maricopa County
Free Library

LITTLE, BROWN AND COMPANY
Boston Toronto

Books Written and Illustrated by F. Wenderoth Saunders

CROSSROADS OF CONQUERORS

BUILDING BROOKLYN BRIDGE

MACHINES FOR YOU

Illustrated by F. Wenderoth Saunders

MY FIRST GEOGRAPHY OF THE PANAMA CANAL

by Arensa Sondergaard

COPYRIGHT © 1967 BY F. WENDEROTH SAUNDERS

ALL RIGHTS RESERVED. NO PART OF THIS BOOK MAY BE REPRODUCED IN ANY FORM OR BY ANY ELECTRONIC OR MECHANICAL MEANS INCLUDING INFORMATION STORAGE AND RETRIEVAL SYSTEMS WITHOUT PERMISSION IN WRITING FROM THE PUBLISHER, EXCEPT BY A REVIEWER WHO MAY QUOTE BRIEF PASSAGES IN A REVIEW.

LIBRARY OF CONGRESS CATALOG CARD NO. 67-17293

FIRST EDITION

Published simultaneously in Canada
by Little, Brown & Company (Canada) Limited

PRINTED IN THE UNITED STATES OF AMERICA

Contents

The author gratefully acknowledges the help of Pauline C. Saunders; J. Ward Carter, Executive Secretary to the Board of Selectmen, Weston, Massachusetts; John J. Carlson, Commissioner of Public Works, Brookline, Massachusetts; and Ralph W. Field, President of Field Machinery Company.

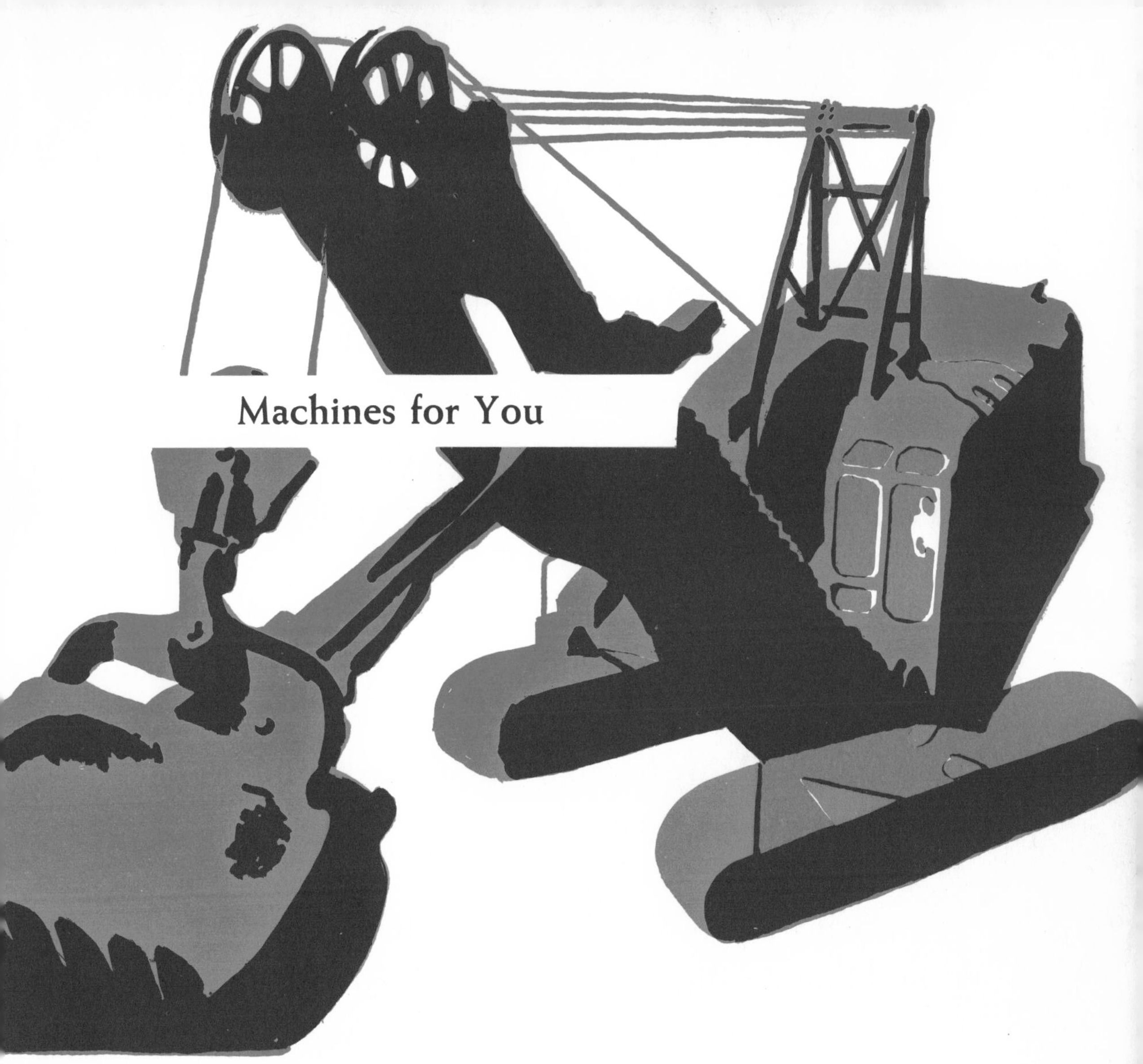

Machines for You

EVERYBODY likes to watch big machines at work. The monsters roar and spit blue smoke like clanking dragons, and they can do the work of a hundred men in half the time.

Maybe you have watched a giant power shovel tear great chunks of earth from the ground like a hungry animal, and then empty its huge jaw, dripping sand and stones, into a waiting dump truck.

Did you want to climb into the control cab to pull the levers that sent the big cat forward or backward, or lift and lower the arm that did the work?

Are these big machines important to you? Are they important to your town? Could you get along without them and live the way you do?

In grandfather's day hand labor, with the help of animals, dug holes, moved earth and piled stones. Now many more things have to be done much faster to build and care for all the homes, roads and community centers that a city or town depends on.

Today big machines keep your town clean and make it a healthy place to live. They prepare land for buildings by digging cellars, mixing concrete and lifting great beams. They help to string wires, prune or move trees. They help to build the great highways so you can travel anywhere in an automobile, and they keep those highways and streets clear for traffic in all seasons.

If your family pays either rent or taxes in your town, you own a small part of the big machines. The

town buys them for you with its tax money. Your town's machines are marked on the sides with the name of the town and the sign HIGHWAY DEPARTMENT or SANITATION DEPARTMENT. They are usually painted a bright orange or yellow or red so that drivers can see them easily and know they must pass by carefully because men and machines are working.

I Machines for Fall

WHEN you go to school in the fall, the first of your town's machines you may see is the *Leaf-sucker-up*. People rake the bright-colored oak and maple leaves from their lawns into the gutters. Then the Leaf-sucker-up, humming loudly and merrily, comes along to suck up the leaves and blow them into an attached truck. This machine is just a huge vacuum cleaner, and the truck is like the dirt bag on a cleaner.

Sometimes instead of the Leaf-sucker-up a fussy, swishy *Street Sweeper* picks up leaves and dirt, or bits of leaves left by the Leaf-sucker-up. The Street Sweeper has strong prickly bristle brushes spinning round and round at high speed. They sweep the dirt against plates called deflectors, which in turn guide the dirt up into a big box known as the hopper. On leaves that are dry and light the Leaf-sucker-up works much better than the Street Sweeper.

To finish the job and make the street nice and clean, a *Street Flusher* waddles into action, dripping water like a fat hippopotamus coming out of a river. The Street Flusher is really a large water tank on wheels. It has three spray nozzles, one on the front and one on each side, big enough to spray half the street at a time. When the water runs off into the drains at the sides of the street, it carries with it the dust left by the Street Sweeper or the Leaf-sucker-up.

Did I say finish the job? Sometimes, but not always. Water pouring into a drain, especially in the fall, may pile up dirt and soggy leaves until the drain is plugged and no more water can run into the sewers. Then a machine called a *Sewer Cleaner* comes to the rescue. Men remove the heavy iron guard grating from the drain, and the Sewer Cleaner reaches out its crane arm, lowers its catch-basin bucket down into the drain, and lifts the dripping muck into a truck. When the last of the slimy mud is pulled out, the grating is put back, and the Sewer Cleaner goes off looking for another clogged drain to clean.

If you live where it snows in winter, your town has to be sure its drains are clear before the snow comes. Sometimes heavy muck gets too deep down in the sewer for the Sewer Cleaner to reach. Then a *Back Hoe*

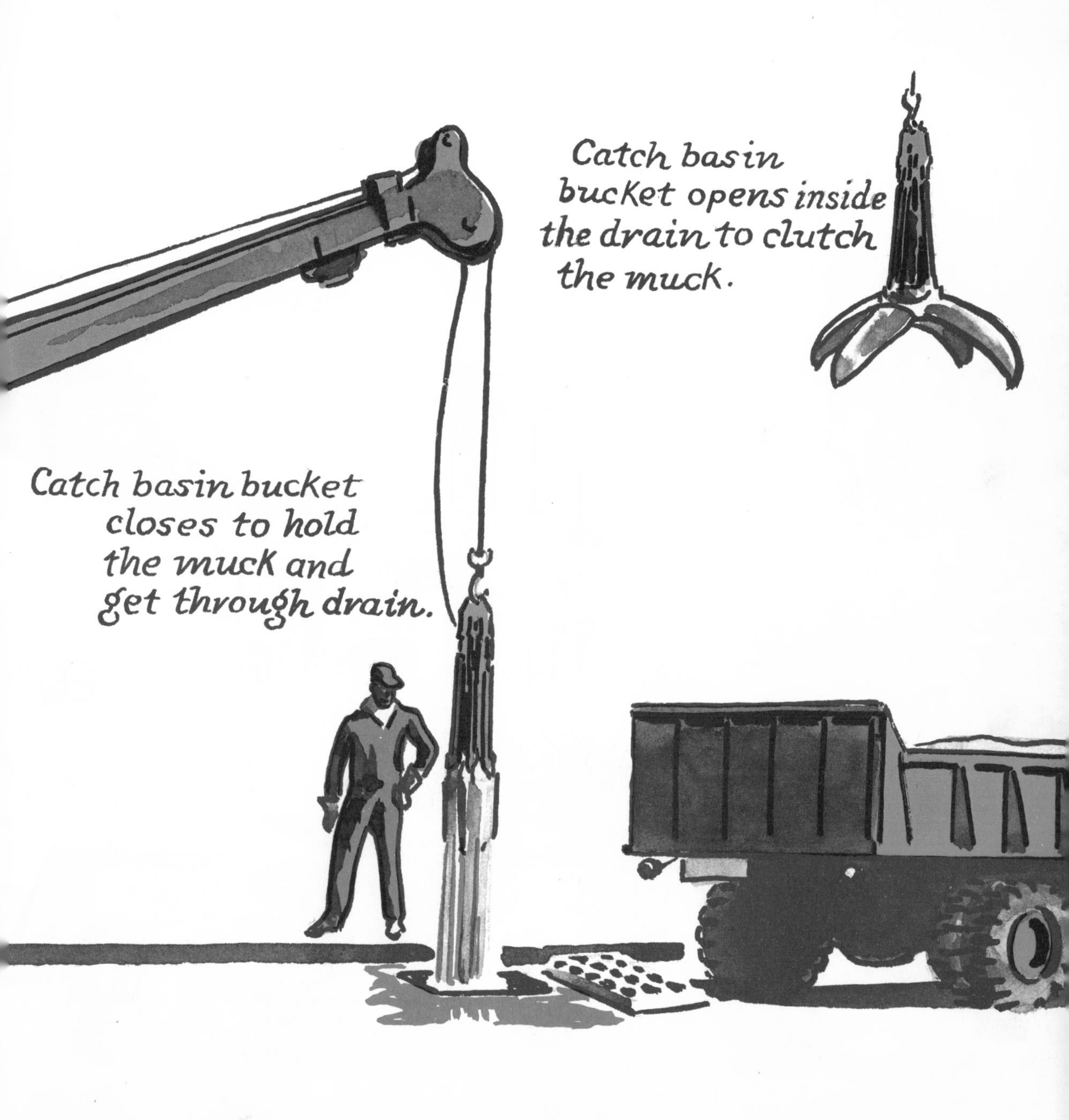

digs up the sewer pipes, and if the pipes are too heavy for men to lift a crane must move them. The Back Hoe is so called because the digging arm is fastened to the rear of the machine. The driver has to sit in another seat to work the hoe. Notice that the machine puts down stabilizers to brace itself just the way you spread your feet when you want to lift something heavy.

II Machines for Winter

WHEN snow does fall, your town must have a whole army of machines ready to fight it. And that is just what snow means for the machines – a battle! Snow, pretty to look at, light and feathery, makes good snowballs and is fine to coast on. But when it deepens, cars can't buck through it, and winds whip it across roads in hard-packed drifts. It melts, then freezes, turning to ice on which autos skid and smash into trees or each other.

If your town could not keep its roads open, everything would come to a full stop. Businesses would shut down, schools and hospitals would close, and you could not get to the stores for food. So the highway department must be ready to fight. *Snow Plows* are its first line of defense. Every town truck of any size carries a steel rig on the front, to which a Snow Plow can be fastened.

At the first warning of snow from the weather bureau, the plows are bolted on the trucks. When only a few inches of snow have fallen, the Snow Plows start out. As long as snow falls, the plows work up one side of a street or highway and back the other side, street after street, each truck plowing its own section of town.

As the snow deepens, a wing or extra blade can be attached to the curb side of the plow. This blade helps the plow push new snow higher at the side of the road.

Snow Plows do not clear all the snow from the surface of the street. If they did, they might rip up the pavement. Snow that is left is quickly packed into ice by cars passing over it. *Sanders,* trucks with spreading machinery, now join the battle. Run by a separate engine at the side of the truck, an endless belt carries a mixture of salt and sand to the rear of the truck where it spills out over a spinning disk or wheel. The spinning disk spreads the salt-sand evenly over one half the road at a time. The sand keeps cars from skidding, while the salt melts the ice.

Some towns — where snows are heavy — have big trucks that do nothing but fight snow. They are called *Snow Fighters*. These are really big battlewagons. Weighing 20 tons or more, each Snow Fighter has a plow on the front, a wide scraper blade in the middle of the truck to pick up what the plow misses and a sand spreader on the rear. Loaded with 10 tons of sand and salt, the Snow Fighter is usually more than a match for the snow armies of King Winter.

There are times when King Winter fights back savagely. Should one snowfall quickly follow another, even the Snow Fighters can't always push snow higher at the side of the road. The hard-packed snow just tumbles back into the roadway. To meet this emergency, engineers invented a *Snow Blower* which can be attached to a truck. The little machines people use

to clear their driveways were patterned after it. The Snow Blower has a set of curved blades on the front, called an auger, which go round and round biting into the snow and lifting it so it can be blown by a continual blast of air from a powerful fan some distance beyond the side of the road.

So where people live close together, after a storm town highway departments clear off the snow piled high by plows at the sides of streets. With the help of still other machines they get ready for King Winter's next attack. One of these machines is the *Snow Loader.* Its long neck makes it look something like a giraffe, but whoever heard of a giraffe in snow country? The auger on the front chews up snow and lifts it onto an endless belt which carries it up the giraffe's neck and spills it down into a waiting dump truck.

Another machine used to clear snow is the *Front End Loader*. It either scoops up snow and lifts it into a dump truck or drops great piles of snow in the path of a Snow Loader.

One machine you really ought to see. The *Snow Melter* is a whale of a machine! Being 47 feet long, it is as big as some whales. And it acts like a whale, with a wide mouth, throat, and great stomach. This enormous creature gobbles up banked snow — 150 tons an hour!

The Snow Melter rumbles and shakes, spits, steams and hisses as it eats its way through the snow. Its cab looks like the cockpit of a big jet liner because of all its gauges and dials. The Snow Melter has four engines too, but each engine does something different. One engine moves the giant. Another turns the auger on the front and the endless belt that carries snow into the stomach of the beast. Still another fires the boiler

where a raging hot flame melts the snow almost instantly, while a fourth pumps melted snow water out through four big faucets or valves into hoses which pour the hot water down street drains.

Not many towns can afford the $90,000 that the Snow Melter costs, but the machine does do the work of many men and smaller machines.

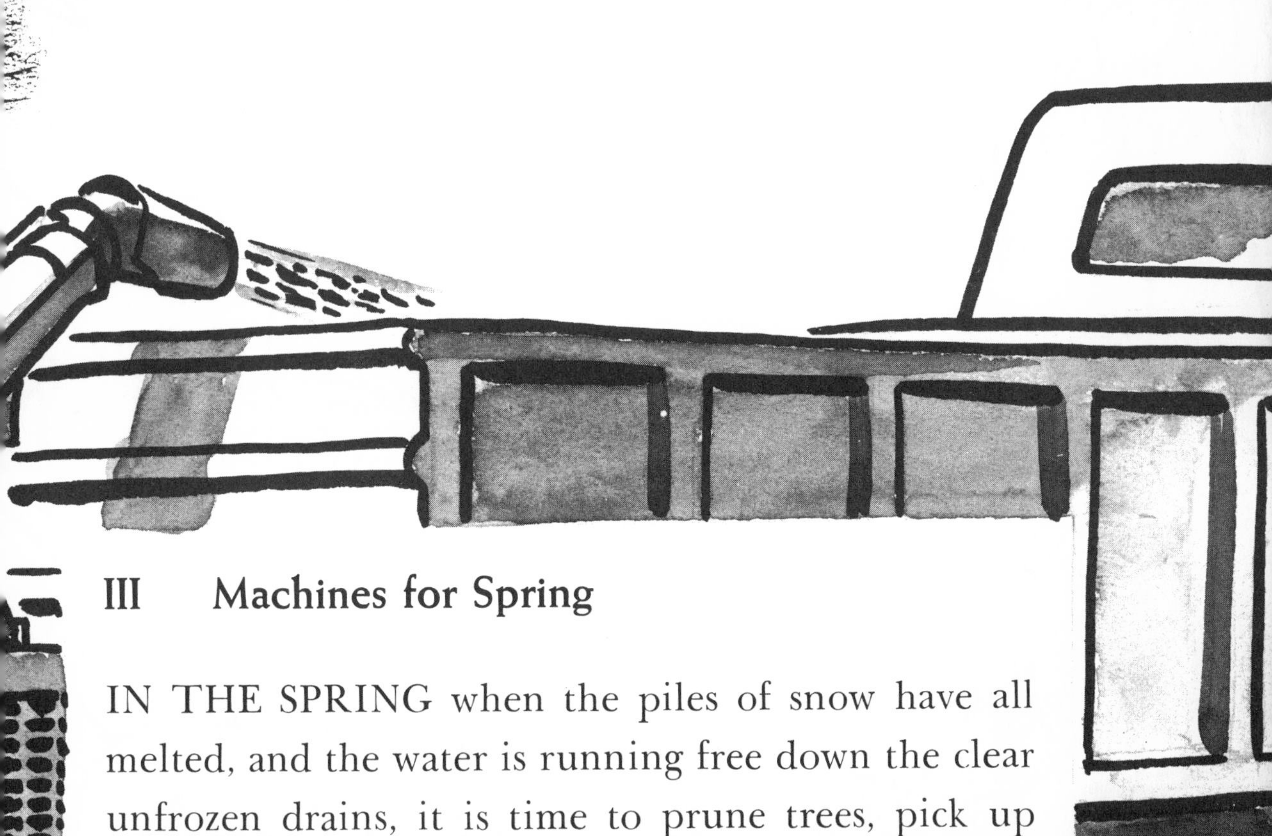

III Machines for Spring

IN THE SPRING when the piles of snow have all melted, and the water is running free down the clear unfrozen drains, it is time to prune trees, pick up broken branches, and tidy parks and roadsides. At home your mother calls it "spring cleaning." The out-of-doors needs cleaning up after a long winter just as much as your own home. This is the time for the *Branch Chipper.*

A Branch Chipper on a truck at the side of a road, gnashing its teeth as it grinds into little pieces the dead branches fed to it by a highway department crew, makes you think of the giant in the nursery rhyme:

Fe, fi, fo, fum,
I smell the blood of an Englishman!
Be he live or be he dead,
I'll grind his bones
To make my bread.

After the Branch Chipper grinds the bones of bushes and trees, it blows the tiny pieces into a truck. One truck can carry what it would take a dozen trucks to haul away if the branches were uncut.

As warmer weather and rains come, grass grows in the parks, at the sides of roads, and in the "medians" – the middle strips of highways. *Tractors* with gang *Lawnmowers* attached can cut long areas of grass each day. For weeds at the sides of roads Tractors with *Cutterbars,* big saw teeth sliding back and forth on a long knife-like steel bar, neatly cut weed stalks close to the ground, doing the work of many men using scythes. This is the same machine that farmers use to cut down fields of hay.

Early spring is also a good time to transplant, that is, to move bushes and trees from one place to another. Large bushes and trees could not be moved without *Cranes*. A big Crane can pick up a big tree and even carry it to a new location, because a Crane is either on wheels or on caterpillar treads.

Maricopa County
Free Library

To prepare a tree for moving, men dig around its roots and a Crane pulls up its trunk. Then the men wrap pieces of heavy cloth around the roots and the dirt clinging to them, so the roots won't be exposed to air and dry out, which would kill the tree.

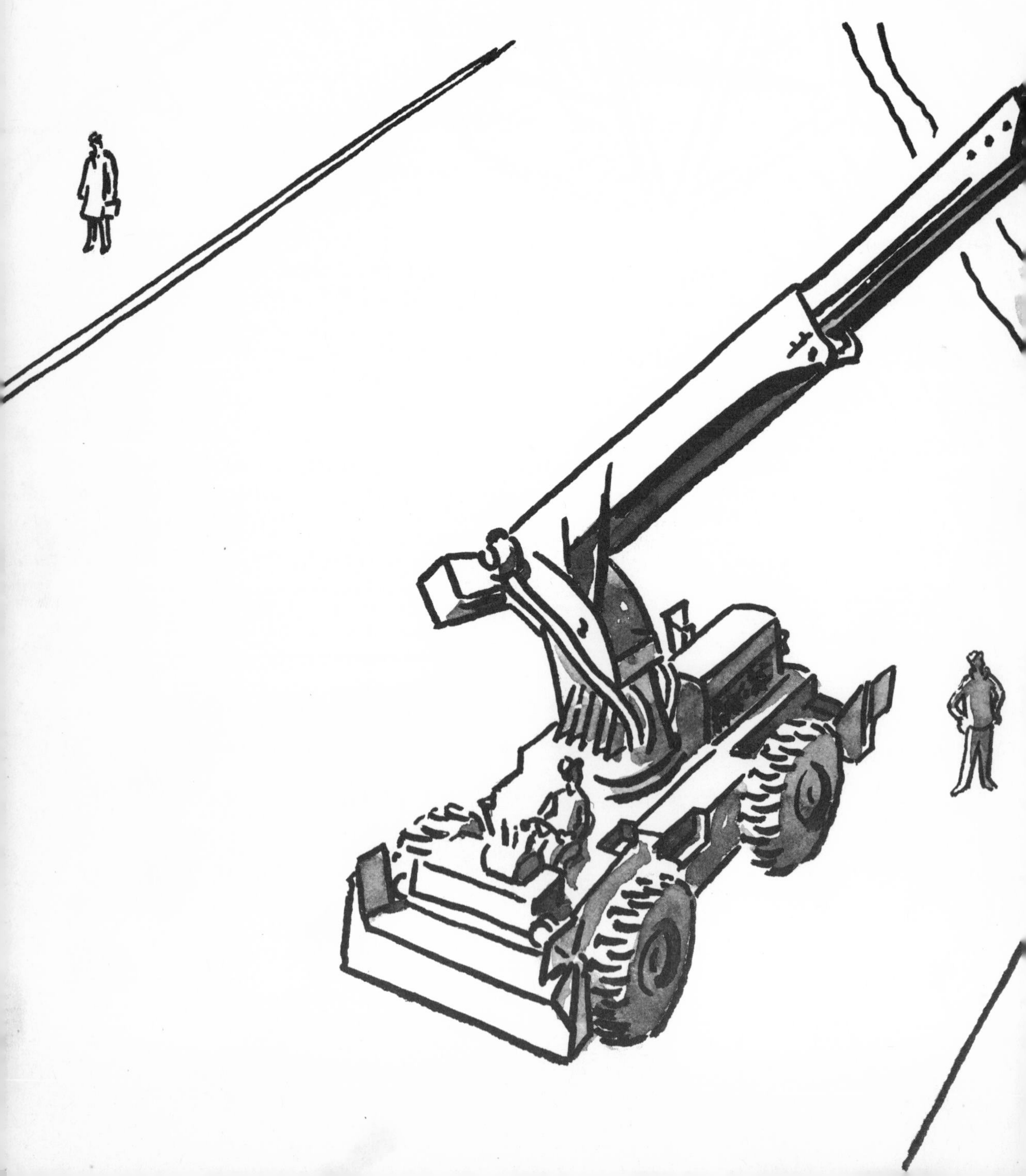

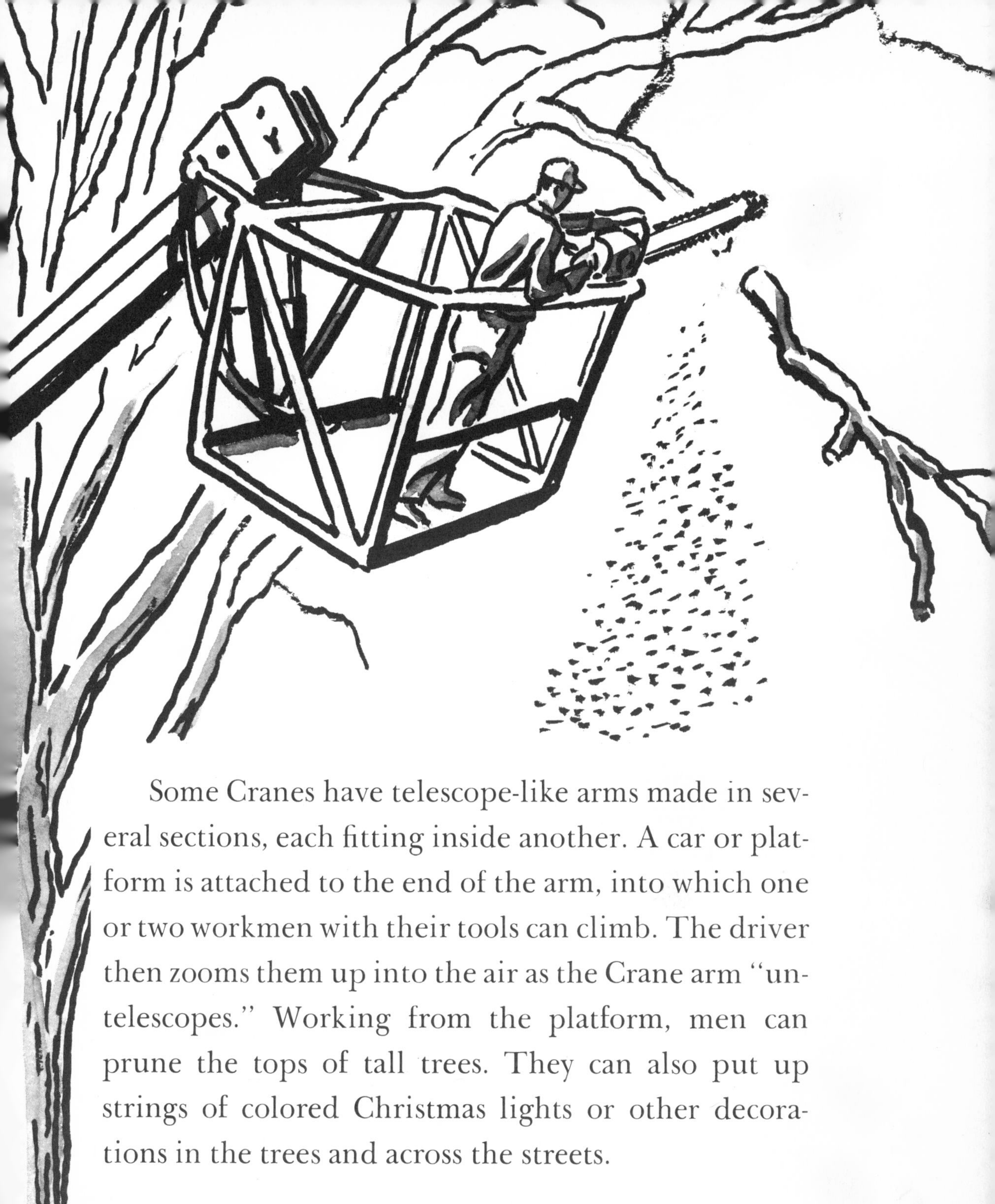

Some Cranes have telescope-like arms made in several sections, each fitting inside another. A car or platform is attached to the end of the arm, into which one or two workmen with their tools can climb. The driver then zooms them up into the air as the Crane arm "untelescopes." Working from the platform, men can prune the tops of tall trees. They can also put up strings of colored Christmas lights or other decorations in the trees and across the streets.

A Crane is one of our most useful machines, and it is among the very oldest, too. An ancestor of the modern Crane worked on the Great Pyramid of Pharaoh Khufu in ancient Egypt nearly 5000 years ago. Cranes are likely to be working the year round in your town.

IV Machines for Spring, Summer, and Fall

AS SOON as the ground is dry in late spring, road building begins. It continues through the summer and into the fall. Perhaps your town will open a new section by building some streets for new houses. Or maybe your town will do its share to build a new highway to keep speeding traffic away from homes and shopping centers. Whether your highway department does the building or hires a private road construction company to do the work, an entirely new team of special machines will go into action.

First engineers survey the land and mark off where the road will go. Next this marked-off area must be cleared of rocks, trees, tangled vines, grass and everything covering the ground. The machine for this job is the great roaring *Bulldozer,* named after one of the most powerful of animals, the bull. The secret of its great strength is the caterpillar treads.

Have you ever tried to push a real caterpillar over? This is practically impossible because there is so much of him on the ground. An inventor studying the underside of a caterpillar noticed that the worm pulled itself along by a series of ridges, all touching the ground at once. Engineers applied this idea to bulldozers, army tanks, and to any machine that has to do a great deal of pushing or has to brace itself firmly on the ground. If you want to turn a machine with caterpillar treads, you shut off power from one tread and give power to the other on the side you want to turn.

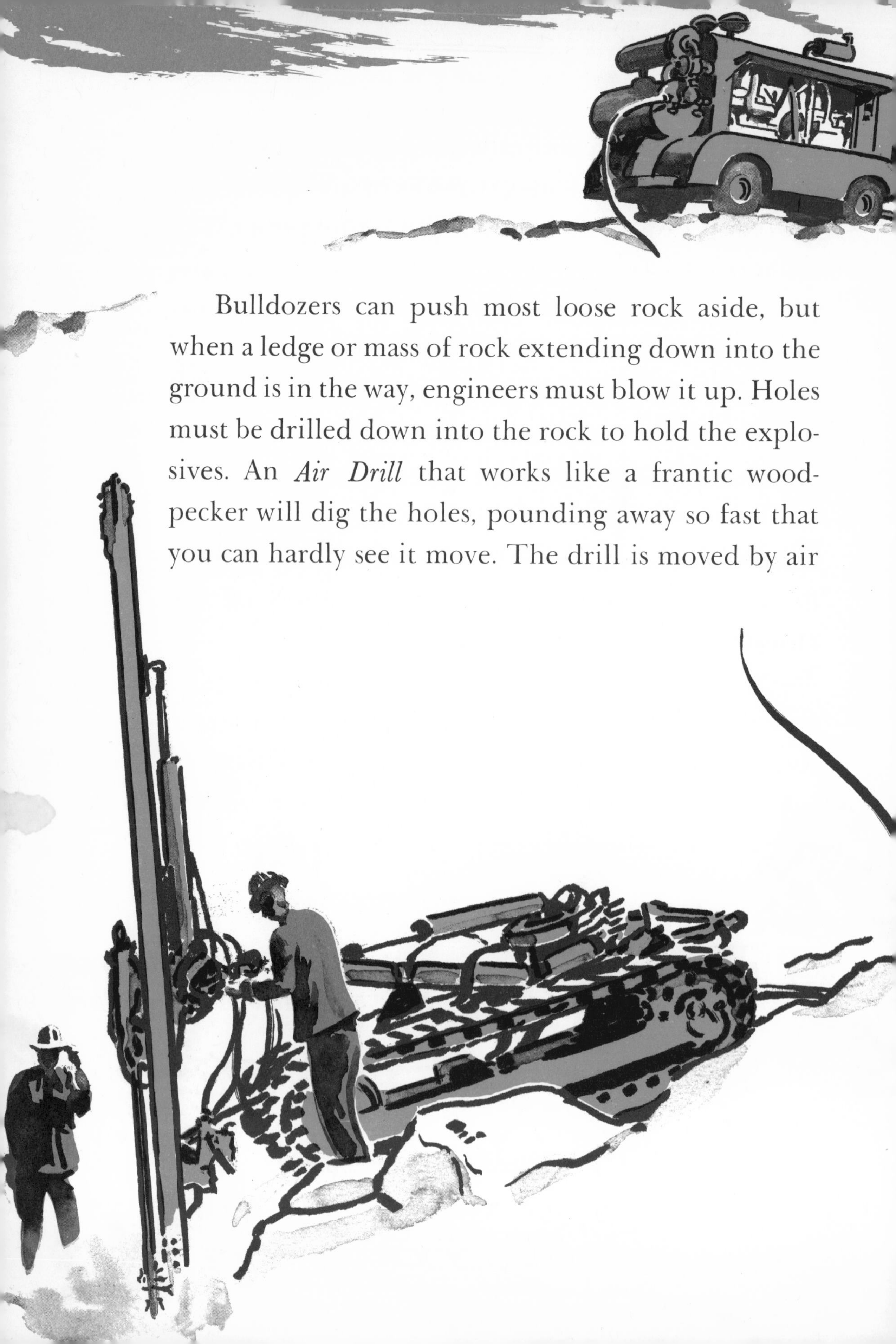

Bulldozers can push most loose rock aside, but when a ledge or mass of rock extending down into the ground is in the way, engineers must blow it up. Holes must be drilled down into the rock to hold the explosives. An *Air Drill* that works like a frantic woodpecker will dig the holes, pounding away so fast that you can hardly see it move. The drill is moved by air from a separate machine called a *Compressor*. The Compressor works on the idea that lots of air squeezed or compressed into a tiny space makes lots of power. You often see Air Drills and Compressors being used also to break up old pavements, perhaps to get at pipes beneath them.

When the required number of holes have been dug and filled with explosives, they are wired electrically together so they will all explode at once. You can bet that the man who touches them off is a good distance away from the ledge. By pushing the plunger down in the control box an engineer sets off the charge.

Probably the engineers will use the rock shattered by the explosives to fill in a low place in the road that they are building. So they call for a *Power Shovel,* mightiest machine of all. Notice that this giant walks on caterpillar treads, also. It empties rock into a rugged truck which is the biggest of its kind. It can hold 120 tons of rock. That is the weight of 40 automobiles!

With all obstacles out of the way and the roadway stripped to bare ground, *Earthscrapers* hurry to scrape off the bumps and ridges and carry away the scrapings to be dumped into low places. An Earthscraper looks like an overgrown lizard with a little head and a great big body. Though it seems small, it houses a powerful, roaring diesel engine. And, just like a lizard, the Earthscraper can scurry away fast with a full load on tires that are higher than a man.

It would save a lot of time and money if the finished surface could be put on the road right after the Earthscrapers have done their job. But tank trucks, furniture vans, cement mixers and all the big boys that

haul a thousand and one things would smash the new surface in a few days. To make a solid base for the finished top, *Dump Trucks* with their bodies tilted to just the right angle spread first a thick layer of broken stone and then a thick layer of gravel.

Then a daddy longlegs of a machine, a giant *Grader*, uses its heavy blade, which the driver can turn at any angle, to level off the layers of broken stone and gravel.

To make sure that everything is solid and packed down hard, a *Compactor,* a lumbering rumbling roller with flat-end spikes, is driven back and forth over the graded undersurface. After its first trip the road looks like one continuous waffle ready for the syrup on top.

If it is a first-class highway there are two kinds of "syrup" you can put on. Engineers call one kind reinforced concrete, the other asphalt. A reinforced concrete road takes careful preparation.

Workmen begin by laying down outer guard rails. Inside this frame other workmen lay a network of steel rods, the reinforcement. This strengthens the concrete that will be the surface.

Concrete is a mixture of sand, water and cement. The cement sticks the mixture together as it dries out. In just the right amounts these three ingredients are put into a huge tank truck. As the tanker heads for

the road under construction, the tank revolves slowly, and by the time the truck arrives, the ingredients are mixed into concrete ready to pour. Since the concrete is mixed on the way or "in transit," the tank trucks are called *In-transit-mixers.*

In-transit-mixers follow each other in endless procession and slide their loads as evenly as possible under and over the reinforcing rods. Then, riding the outer guard rails, comes the *Concrete Paver* which easily packs and smoothes the still wet concrete.

If concrete dries out too quickly on top and before the underneath can dry, the surface will crack. So men follow the Paver, and spread straw or cloth over the wet concrete. These coverings are kept wet with hoses for a day or two so the whole mass of concrete will dry evenly.

Asphalt, the other road surface, is a mixture of heavy oil and sand heated together. Nature makes asphalt, too. There is a whole lake of it in the West Indian island of Trinidad. The first asphalt roads in this country were made from this thick Trinidad

mud, but men learned how to imitate nature and make asphalt at home, which is cheaper.

Dump Trucks bring hot asphalt directly to the job from the plant where it is made. Each truck as it is needed backs up to the hopper of the *Asphalt Paver,* and the body of the truck is tilted so just the right amount of asphalt will feed out slowly. Moving by its own power the Paver pushes the truck ahead. An endless belt in the Paver carries the asphalt to the rear where it is spread evenly and smoothly over one lane of the highway at a time.

The first asphalt roads were not very satisfactory, for asphalt is soft and sticky stuff in hot weather. Railroad tracks on the Trinidad asphalt lake have to be

moved frequently or they would sink right out of sight. In the summer, people left footprints on the new roads, and the first autos put ruts in the surface. To prevent this, engineers mixed in more sand, and invented big *Power Rollers* that press the surface hard. Since asphalt is black, and black absorbs heat, dry powdered cement was brushed over the road just after it had been rolled, to whiten the top. White reflects hot sunlight and keeps the road cooler and therefore harder.

On country roads where there is little heavy traffic a *Tar Spreader,* which looks and acts something like our friend the Street Flusher, spreads a coat of shining black tar over half the road at a time. A gas flame underneath the Spreader keeps the tar hot enough to spread. After the Tar Spreader has passed, men shovel sand on the tar. Traffic passing over this mixture soon makes a solid coat of tar and sand, but not before a country boy can walk in it and track tar on the rugs in his house – and be punished for it!

No highway is complete without guide lines, so that drivers of autos will follow the first rule of the road, "Keep to the right." To make these lines quickly and evenly someone invented a machine, the *Line Painter*. Lines are mighty helpful at night or in fog when you can hardly see anything of the road ahead.

Man in Trailer controls flow of paint which is spread through 1, 2 or 3 nozzles by compressed air from a compressor. The man in the cab who drives the truck tells the Trailer Man by intercom when to paint the center white guide line and the "no passing" orange lines. Little flecks of glass are spread with the paint to make the lines glow at night.

Paint Tanks white, orange

Trailer

It would be hard to walk along a street if automobiles were parked right up to the fronts of stores, or if water after a heavy rain could run like a river along the walk. To keep automobiles and water in their proper places in a street, raised sidewalks edged with curbs make it possible to walk safely and easily.

The first curbs were either quarried from stone or molded in forms from concrete. Now a machine, the *Curb Maker,* comes along and neatly makes curbs and puts them in place all at one time.

Some of the big machines that are used to make streets and roads help us to build houses, schools, libraries, hospitals, factories and other structures. In the late spring when Bulldozers go to work on roads, other Bulldozers clear land for buildings. *Powerdozers,* which are Bulldozers on big wheels instead of cater-

pillar treads, clear land faster because they can move faster, but the Powerdozer can't push as hard as the Bulldozer if the job is tough. Back Hoes dig cellar holes while Power Shovels dig basements of bigger buildings.

If the land where a big building is to be erected is swampy, with no solid place for the building to stand, it is necessary to drive long thick posts called piles down into the ground until they reach rocky ledge. The foundation will then be built on the piles. A giant Crane keeps dropping a heavy weight, like a hammer driving a nail, on the end of the pile until it is down

DISCARD

to the basement level. Likewise, when an old building has to be torn down, a Crane may knock it to pieces with a steel or concrete ball.

In climates where the ground freezes, water pipes, drains and sewer pipes must be put down below frost level. Back Hoes dig trenches for pipes, and if the pipes are heavy, Cranes pick up and lower the pipes into place. In fact Cranes stay right on the job to lift up steel girders, beams and heavy construction materials as buildings rise on their foundations.

V Machines the Year Around

SOME MACHINES work for us all the time – in rain, snow, heat, cold, on good days and bad days. These are the machines that remove refuse and garbage. By coming every week at least, these machines help keep your yard and house clean. They make your town a healthful place to live by taking away dirt and filth that could breed disease.

Have you helped your father set out the trash cans filled with dry rubbish of all sorts, such as paper, cans, jars, and rags? The *Refuse Truck* drives down the middle of the street while a crew of men pick up the trash cans from both sides and empty them into a wide mouth at the rear of the truck.

An endless belt carries the trash and stuffs it into the covered hopper of the truck. Some towns have their Refuse Trucks empty the waste into big open-air pits where it is burned, but if people live near, they will dislike the smoky smudge the burning trash makes.

Larger towns and cities send trash along with garbage to incinerators. An incinerator is a tremendous furnace used just to burn up waste. A tall smokestack empties the little smoke that is left high in the air and provides a strong draft or current of air that makes the fire hot enough to burn up everything but metal and glass.

Garbage Trucks work pretty much the same way as Refuse Trucks except that there is usually less garbage than trash, and therefore the Garbage Truck has to make fewer trips to the incinerator for the number of houses it serves.

We say a machine is highly specialized if it is made to do just one thing, like a Curb Maker or a Line Painter or a Leaf-sucker-up. The *Refuse Dumpster* belongs in this class, also. If you owned a store, you would put your trash in one giant box which is as big as some small rooms. The Refuse Dumpster would bring an empty box just the same size, put it down behind your store, and pick up your full box to take it to the incinerator. The box is so large that one box is a full load for the Refuse Dumpster.

If you add fire engines and police vehicles to all the machines we have talked about, you can see what a large amount of equipment a town has to use. Your town has to own machines which the town uses all the time. Other machines, used only occasionally, your town rents from private owners called contractors. Sometimes a town will turn a whole job over to a contractor and say, "Here, you do it!"

In this case your town will first say what the job is, what materials must go into it, and how the work must be done. Contractors bid for the job – they say how much money they will charge to do the work. They put their bids in sealed envelopes, and hand them to the town engineer, who opens them all together on a certain day. This gives everybody a fair chance. The job goes to the contractor who bids the lowest sum of money for doing the work. Then it is up to the town engineer to see that the contractor does just what the town wants done.

Machines and town work cost a great deal of money, but if it makes your town a safer and more comfortable place to live, the money is well spent.

Index